THE NEAR AND FAR

THE NEAR AND FAR

Poems by Jody Bolz

Turning Point Books

Published by Turning Point Books
P.O. Box 541106
Cincinnati, Ohio 45254

Poetry Editor: Kevin Walzer
Business Editor: Lori Jareo

Visit us at www.turningpointbooks.com

ISBN: 9781625493255

Cover and book design by Carol Beehler

Cover photo by Paul Barbera
from his series "The Girl from Ipanema"

ACKNOWLEDGMENTS

Grateful acknowledgment is made to the following publications, in which these poems first appeared:

5 A.M: "The Lost Hour"
Beltway Poetry Quarterly: "The Words We Say"
Indiana Review: "Shadow of the Family" (as *"Sombra de la Familia"*)
Manhattan Review: "How the Past Appeared"
MiPOesias: "Echo"
Moment: "Storm Watch," "The World Starts"
North American Review: "Evening"
Poetic Voices without Borders (Robert Giron, ed.), Gival Press: "Speak to Water"
Poetry East: "A Cold Day in Late March," "Drift," "February Morning," "Passage," "Tableau," "Threshold," and "Visitation"
Poetry Quarterly: "Mockingbird" (as "Night Singing") and "Night Sounds"
Poets and Artists: "The House Itself"
Praxilla: "Last Frame"
Southern Poetry Review: "A Marriage," "Deadfall," "First Marriage," "Hindsight," "Ice," "Late at Night the Lightning," "Repairs," "Shade Garden," "The Near and Far"
To Woo & to Wed (M. Blumenthal, ed.), Poseidon Press: "Driving Home in Two Cars"

Many thanks to Kate Blackwell, Genevieve DeLeon, Samantha Guerry, Linda Pastan, Jane Shore, and Leslie Ullman for their careful attention to many of these poems as they were being written. — J.B.

For Brad—with me, near and far

CONTENTS

I. HINDSIGHT

II. THE NEAR AND FAR

You can call on beauty still and it will leap
from all directions

You can write beauty into the cruel file
of things done   things left undone

—ADRIENNE RICH

THE NEAR AND FAR

I. HINDSIGHT

Deadfall

Not the fallen tree
but the falling, uncanny,
across the road ahead:

first, a high shimmer
on the periphery,
as if the crown

were caught in wind,
and then the swoon—
leaf-tips, twigs, branches

collapsing in succession
before the trunk's weight.
Was it a mulberry? An oak?

There wasn't time to look.
I had to brake—turn back.
And I did. I could.

It was a matter of seconds,
a matter of yards.
I don't know why it didn't scare me.

Instead, I found it beautiful
and sad—like chance
itself. Like safety.

First Marriage

Today the sky's
gone dark
in early afternoon.

A flash—a rolling boom—
and the inside lights
blink out,

the radio stops—
a prosperous vacancy
before the rain begins,

all the engines
of the built world
giving up,

and no sound but the storm
with its bearable
wreckage.

I've been thinking
of another day's
changeable weather,

outside the county
courthouse where we traveled
to get married.

Only after we'd signed in
and were waiting
to say our vows

did the storm start
in earnest. We turned
to the window

and saw there, hanging
from the brick façade,
a stuttering neon rainbow.

A sign! you said,
laughing—
and then the judge began.

Ice

At dusk I saw a beaver
near a patch of open water
at the mouth of a rill.

It foraged for a while
in the brush along the bank,
then slid into the dark canal,

circled as if summoning its will,
and slipped under the ice—
a thoroughfare of glassy green

that stretched out of sight.
I ran along the towpath,
keeping pace,

transfixed by its shape,
which sped without veering,
not a shadow but a living thing.

For fifty yards or so,
it seemed to disappear where
skates had scarred the surface,

but once the ice came clear,
I found it streaming beside me—
drawing closer to its aim

as I got farther from home.
How far could it go?
Half a mile? More?

Winded—dizzy—
I couldn't look away
until I couldn't see.

The sun was almost down,
cliffs across the river
edged in red.

Weeds froze at my feet.
Evening hardened overhead.
I stepped

onto the ice,
not faithless—not faithful—
and then, I turned back.

Last Frame

Early morning—early March—
I stood on the curb
outside the old apartment,

and watched you leave.
Decades later
it's a simple scene to stage:

a woman, bare-legged
beneath a black wool coat,
shivers in the first light

on a city street,
hair buffeting
her blotchy cheeks,

while a man, trapped
in the stale heat of a taxi,
twists back to see her wave.

His cab rounds a corner
on the far side of the bridge,
and still the woman stays,

staring from the curb
as his distance from her lengthens.
It's only space,

measurable in miles,
but to move now,
to walk into the lobby,

down the dingy hallway
to her door—
to open it, shrug

her coat off,
shower and dress for work—
is to let time start again.

What she can't get past
is how small and sad
his face looked

as the taxi moved away,
how young he seemed—
and frightened—

as if he knew already
that their plans
had come to nothing,

that this blustery morning
with its stripped,
swaying trees,

this figure shrinking
against a new red sky,
was a picture of parting.

Driving Home in Two Cars

This moon isn't like some other thing—
just a moon, four or five days old
but bright enough I've got to squint to see it all.
I look a second time, then back to the road
to find the car I'm following is gone.

Down through foothills,
not knowing the way home,
I imagine the baby sagging toward her thumb,
my husband turning back to talk to our son,
radio yawning and sputtering on
as their wheels slip the embankment...

I gun the engine, round three curves
and nearly rear-end them.
Out of breath, we start again.

Not porch lights, not nightlights,
just taillights: still I train
my half-sad love on these red points.
An old van passes,
slips briefly in between,

as if nothing joins us.
Near dawn one night, unable to sleep,
I tracked my husband breath for breath,
determined to catch up.
And though I couldn't,
though I didn't,
I wouldn't give up until he woke.

Listening to our children
whirring in their beds—distinct
from each other, distinct
from us—I've wished away their bodies,

wished away our own,
as if that would bring us home.

This is almost it:
a year-old boy opens a book
to his favorite page
(magic to him, magic to him),
sets it on the floor,
stands on it,
waits,
then breaks into tears.

Farmhouses with Christmas trees
stream on the periphery,
the moon starts its slide
down a slough of stars.

I watch the taillights of our car.

Shadow of the Family

No matter how large the house,
how green its walls,
how various its blossoms
or how small, brown
and gardenless—
at night each is a point
on the terrain: a brief remark
lit up and obscured,
different from the address
its family claims on documents,
different from the scent of its halls,
the isolating histories of its air.

Drive anywhere—
through the tropics, say,
in central Costa Rica
on unpaved roads,
past hills on fire on purpose,
past schools that are pavilions
awash by daybreak
in blue and white uniforms,
past rivers and lagoons,
the tag-ends of uncultivated palms,
where even toucans are colorless
in the equatorial dark:

Drive out or drive back,
toward or away from some hope,
some place with chances,
and you'll think about
all the homes of all the people
you will never meet,
their positions on the land,
their proximity to or distance from
the road, their very stasis
relative as your own movement

(race of a shadow below a big moon)—
yet what conviction it offers.

And you are hard to see
as all their roofs and porches,
your passage reducible to headlights
moving north, however complete
you may imagine yourself—
you *have* imagined yourself,
walking a lamp-lit street with your love,
the baby on your shoulders,
boy on his, all four fixed
within a single silhouette:
a kingdom whose partitioning
anyone can chart.

Speak to Water

In the seconds before his pebble
thwaps well water,
how many feet below,
startling the air all around him,
startling him,
the child looks down in,
says hello

lolololo.

I would speak to water
if I believed
water listens,
instead of half-believing,

if I thought my own reflection
no mere play of light
but a rejoinder,
transparent and dazzling,

if it were true
to my intentions,
truer than the voices
I love but misconstrue,
direct as an echo
and more transforming,

something to make me look again
at my own claim,
the posture it suggests,
something to make
every beauty possible,
if not by magic
then by clarity and motion.

I would speak
if I could learn from water
anything like patience:
the steady force of it.

The Words We Say

In love there is a logic of gestures
we don't interpret but trust,
a courtship outlasting
our beauty and our grief:

your face at rest above a book,
your hand rising across the yard
suggesting a hedge—a summerhouse—
or dropping flat-palmed to your chest.

A turning away in sleep,
a turning back.
We learn from it for years,
approach one another,

wave like infants as we meet
or throw off the embrace,
afraid to be tested, afraid as if
we could do more than this,

give more than this—the body's
full tilt, undisguised and honorable,
and the full light of attention—
as if to press our skulls against each other's,

water birds eye-to-eye, were not enough—
as if we could make love transform us,
never fall away, separate
as the words we say and mean.

A Cold Day in Late March

Spring begins in increments,
like knowledge

or despair. The year
opens its hands,

a deft green gesture,
and grass appears.

Sleet flattens it, but
not for long.

Why does it surprise me?
I look at you now

as if you were assembling
before my eyes.

As if you were vanishing.
Your smile starts—

not pageantry, not yet—
or your face goes slack.

We were married
on a day like this,

just after the snowstorm
nobody foresaw.

How many times
have we told the story?

Our relief when the guests
arrived, steering down

the narrow road once
deadfall had been cleared.

Sun shifted through the pines,
welcome—welcoming—

and smoke climbed
from the chimneys

of that shabby, stately house.
At sunset we said our vows.

Cold and wet and broken,
limbs remember how to blossom.

April presses in with its
onslaught of promises.

The Lost Hour

What might have happened
didn't happen.

It was raining again
or still raining,

the river at flood-stage
but not yet flooding

while we slept
and woke and slept

in our own bed
at two in the morning,

and I dreamt
I was with strangers

in an unfamiliar city,
staring at a spot-lit stage

when someone behind me
struck a match,

setting me on fire—
coat burning through in back,

flames reaching
for my hair—

but I'm alive
I was thinking,

as if the pain itself
were my responsibility,

something to master,
unable as I was to move

but able at least
to scream,

and you heard me,
placed your hands

on my shoulders,
waking me

to rain at the window
and spring racing in.

How the Past Appeared

It wasn't the wall itself
or its setting on a cliff—

not its width or color,
though the wall did flare

above the path where I walked
an hour before dark,

so that I had to stop and look,
blindsided by a blazing shape,

its windows lacy flames
within a wider fire,

radiance I recognized on sight:
not the building itself

but the way that light
outshone the present moment,

making it unreal, and myself
within it a figure in eclipse,

the urgent past—invisible how long?—
burning above me, and gone.

Hindsight

She looks over
her right shoulder—
long neck curved,

tendons taut—
as if she's just heard
someone say her name.

There's nothing
unfamiliar
about her posture:

a triggered expectancy
both eager and wary,
a look recognizable

in train stations
and city parks.
Woman looking back

or, in this case,
Goddess looking back—
Venus, in fact.

The man who sculpted
her pose
must have died

two thousand years ago,
but even now
the look unfolds:

Love turns back
as if for the first time.
As if she can see.

II. THE NEAR AND FAR

(a sequence)

I • *Tableau*

Tableau

For beauty not for heat we built
fires all winter the small square
of our hearth an altar or a theater
but what were we witnessing
beguiled by the smell and sound

the walls of the living room
billowing around our gold
and shadowed figures image
of a family from another age
the firelight itself unfixed

in time unfixed in place
general as the dark and cold
as hunger and danger though
we were warm and safe
furnace humming radiators hot

to the touch our kitchen stocked
mere steps from where we sat
talking or reading or listening to music
and sometimes the phone rang
or the cats cried to go out

we rarely sat in silence but
imagining it now the only sound
is the bright pulse of the fire
not the pop and hiss of burning just
the airy errant thrumming of the flames

2 • *Night Sounds*

Night Sounds

For thirty years we've slept
together in this room
window cracked open
on your side of the bed even
in winter so we can hear the swish

of snow the rain and wind and sometimes
owls calling tree to tree
or peepers chiming in the swamp nearby
crickets in summer and after thunder
the bristling thud of falling limbs

once in a while we'll startle
to the beeping of a service truck
backing up the wail of an ambulance
answering a call and three times
maybe four a helicopter's shuddering

swoon above the spot-lit river
but most nights almost all we slept
and woke and slept turning towards
and away from one another our faces
barely visible except on full-moon nights

the bed a home inside a home
haven we've returned to
ten thousand times or more
I want to sleep in this room until
I can't sleep anywhere wake in this bed

to find you beside me as I did
on our first morning here
late-November sunlight filtering
through the summer shifts
I'd draped across the windows

my belly huge with the baby
who'd be born three weeks later
but was nameless then
a person inside another person
unready for space and light

for wide-ranging night sounds
unable then to laugh or sob
or wake up in a narrow crib
to call across the rushing dark
his first words his words for us

3 • *The House Itself*

The House Itself

Easy to believe this house
belonged to strangers
before it was ours
but impossible to picture
strangers living here again

waking in this room
and stepping to the window
to gaze out at the Green
a view less open years from now
the redbuds and native oaks

we planted as saplings
grown tall by then grown wide
how quickly it happens
you find a home to settle in
meet neighbors and restore the porch

pull wild vines from every bush
cut ivy from the trees
you jack and shim
the sagging floor in back
of the living room repaint

the walls repair the garage
you buy an old farm table
hampers mirrors chairs
and soon the place is yours
its stairs and shadows

the doorway of each room
your clothes in the closets
your books on the shelves
your fire and your darkness
your infant in your arms

4 • *Passage*

Passage

The upstairs hall is narrow
five strides long and one across
three rooms so close together
that the children could call us
from their beds if they were sick

or scared they didn't have to shout
the four of us were clustered
in the roofline of the house
so we thought the kids felt safe
at least they never had to brave

a long dark corridor to find us
and for years we lived that way
within reach of one another
each bedroom ceiling streaked
with a stanza of deflected light

easy then to feel at home
the place adrift in picture books
and puppets toy animals in cheerful
clothes rag-tag collections
of marbles fir-cones feathers

the local world's offerings of signs
and wonders antique bottles
unearthed in the ravine
white stones round as story moons
objects of enchantment

and weren't we enchanted
though tired and worried
thwarted sometimes grieving
both our fathers sick and dying
in those years we thought would last

but couldn't last of course not
our home a home like that
only for children to grow up in
and then leave crossing
the narrow hall away from us

5 • *Storm Watch*

Storm Watch

Were we on the porch already the baby in her play-pen
boy careening from the hammock to the rocking chair
and back or did we rush out when the storm began
wanting to be almost in it outside but still sheltered
thunder thudding through our ribs the kids spellbound

and abstracted never crying to be held the downpour
only yards away cold spray of spring rain in our hair
and on our faces there was nothing for those minutes
but the green world's shudder and the sky split silver
over our magnolia tree which swooned and beckoned

water pooling at its roots then rushing to the street
the neighbors' houses indistinct though maybe they
were home too standing by the windows looking out
at the four of us a family in a shadow box that gleamed
and dimmed and gleamed again before it went dark

6 • *Evening*

Evening

Most days I cooked without gratitude
standing at the kitchen counter
rinsing and chopping and checking
the clock at five-fifty six-fifteen
the violets on our windowsill

backlit by sunset or outlined
in winter dark as I placed pots
to simmer over wide blue flames
stirring tasting seasoning our food
there was never any question

of whether or when or what
we might eat we had everything
we needed and the fact seemed
commonplace our comfort
commonplace each evening

a steep course to master task by task
scouring the cutting board sponging
the stove-top talking to the children
as they leaned over their worksheets
looking up from time to time to spar

with one another or leaping to the door
to let the cats back in while I watched
the hour pass beyond a wall of windows
seasons in free-fall like the pages
of a flipbook green and gold and gone

sometimes when it snowed the kids
would drop their pencils to race outside
and see but I didn't join them
I was barreling downhill
in the midst of all that beauty

veering through each gate
to be done and done and done
another weekday evening
vanishing beneath me
and now the level ground flung wide

7 • *Intimations*

Intimations

I raise the shades each morning
on a southern magnolia
green in every season
and a mulberry that's bare
four months each year

a vertical thicket
though songbirds return to it
in March not needing leaves
to know it's spring
I've looked at these two trees

so long and still they surprise me
unpredictable as extras
in the foreground of the scene
signaling indifference
vitality distress but only once

in all this time
was there a freezing rain
so gentle and so brief
it sheathed their limbs in ice
turning them to glass

so I dressed and ran outside
to get a closer look
but when I pried the glaze
from a single magnolia leaf
it shattered on my glove

I tried again and again
until I lifted one clear scrim
unbroken from tip to stem
a perfect simulacrum
etched with tiny veins

and since the children were asleep
I carried it across the street
to show our neighbor's son
a boy so young he didn't speak
but reached to touch

the see-through leaf amazed
to watch its near edge shrink
a wondrous shape fallen from a world
where living things go cold
before they disappear

8 • *Shade Garden*

Shade Garden

Not ten years not twelve
maybe fifteen maybe more
I can't remember when
the maple we planted as a sapling
grew so tall it started shading

out the garden but how
could we cut it down
we'd put it in the ground
after our daughter was born
and it was her tree hers

its bark and boughs its starry leaves
we thought instead
we'd redesign the flowerbeds
that once had bloomed
from April through mid-July

we'd scrap the showy daffodils
the red and purple tulips
plump irises as white as doves
and start again with native plants
that thrive in shade

bayberry and spicebush
viburnum glade ferns asters
we'd make a list with sound advice
from seasoned gardeners
so I did I made a list

I made a plan but then
did nothing
changed nothing
never dug up the failing bulbs
and never replanted

it was as if I wouldn't accept
the shade or maybe
I accepted it but couldn't act
couldn't change
and I know it was it is

it always has been my way
not yours my failing
not yours to see what's ruined
and refuse to give it up
to let it go the garden

barely growing now but
ours still ours
its roots and stems
its stubborn vines each last
returning blossom

9 • *Drift*

Drift

Often when I bathe I slide down
in the tub until my neck dips
under water and my chin skims
the surface steam rising around me
as I close my eyes breathe slowly

something I played at as a child
the water's silky warmth a cover
tub a bed until my mother
came in to rinse my hair and swirl
a soapy cloth across my back

what happens now is different
deep and irresistible and sometimes
when I shift I'll be suddenly alert
but unsure where I am
not that I'm in danger I could

right myself if I began to slip
still it baffles me to drift
between consciousness and sleep
our battered tub a kind of grave
containing me exactly

I don't know why I can't focus
on washing up and drying off
don't know why I loll there
listless in a stage-set sea
my limbs as pale as sandbars

why I'm present and absent
in the same room where
we first bathed our infant son
his gray eyes widening before
he trusted water with the air's

sharp chill above it before
he could be sure of my hand
beneath his neck as I ran
a cloth across his chest speaking
to him softly saying his new name

10 • *Repairs*

Repairs

Who's kept track of the broken
things you've fixed over the years
repairs you've made as if they were nothing
never doubting you could figure out
what tools to use what steps to take

why leave a task to someone else
when you can do it or at least
you'll try poring over diagrams
squinting at instructions
driving to the hardware store

twice on a Saturday to gather supplies
brackets for the rattling pipes
copper wire solder spackle
hinges slide-lock thermostat
and items I can't even name

no system in this house
seems alien to you no failure
alarming so why am I surprised
that I've learned next to nothing
understood next to nothing

about heat and light and water
relying on you
to know what's wrong
and find a way to fix it
relying on you never to break

11 • *April Fools*

April Fools

For days we thought the robin
flying at our window
wanted to get in
so we placed a wooden owl
on the ground to scare him off

and when he kept on coming
we figured he'd gone mad
throwing himself
against the panes
in back of the living room

though when we kept
the shade down
hours sometimes passed
between his forays
especially when it rained

but when the sun broke through
there he was again
racing at the window
leaving wing prints on the glass
like lines scrawled in haste

was it slapstick or alarming
we weren't sure how to react
he wasn't injuring himself
or threatening us in any way
we joked as we conspired

against him but as each plot failed
the thud of his body
on the glass began
to unnerve me
his endurance unnerved me

even when I realized
he was doing nothing more
than protecting his patch
from a rival
he couldn't manage

a rival who met each attack
with equal and opposing force
vying with reflections
on his side of the window
just as I was on mine

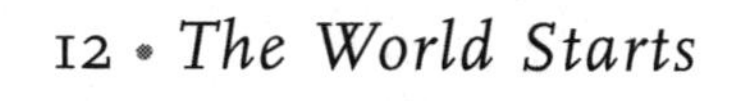

12 • *The World Starts*

The World Starts

Only a child would ask
where the world starts
as if she weren't in it
but I've wondered
I wonder now

when I wrote poems about war
my friend called them
my "world poems"
a kind way to suggest
I'd overstepped

and maybe I had
sometimes I can't tell
what's far from what's near
a suicide bomber
in a Baghdad market

from the poet I found
dead by her own hand
floor soaked through
with her child's blood
with hers

my mistake
unless horror is horror
and delusion delusion
one instance mirroring another
and the mind itself a world

13 • *Visitation*

Visitation

You were traveling for work
as you often were in those years
and it might have been early spring
since we'd been outside all afternoon
with so many neighbors who'd

emerged from their homes
wearing sweaters and garden gloves
or maybe it was fall and I was raking
while the children looped the house
in some improvised game

they were young then
three and five and almost
inexhaustible shouting
to each other as they ran
and at some point a young man

I'd never seen before sauntered
up our walk asking to do yard work
just going door to door
like the guys who sell firewood
weeks before Thanksgiving

when you hadn't even thought
you might be running low
so I said *No thanks not today*
smiling as I spoke
and he argued for a moment

eyes narrow weak jaw set
but once he'd left and I'd turned back
to whatever I'd been doing
I thought it odd he was on foot
and carrying nothing

the day passed a good day
and the three of us were hungry
by the time I served dinner
then I bathed them both
I read to them

and once they were in bed
I went back down
to clean the kitchen
toss the garbage lock the doors
before going to bed myself

knowing you couldn't call
from your faraway time zone
the hours passed we slept
windows open to the breeze
until a sudden commotion

started up in my dream
and I woke heart pounding
to a banging at the door
so I stumbled downstairs
without pulling on a robe

there he was in silhouette
fist on the wooden frame
around the old glass panes
shouting *I need to make a call*
I need money I need help

and even though I was shaking
I stood straight and shouted back
It's the middle of the night
I'll call the police if you don't leave
thinking the whole time

how easy it would be
for him to smash the door
as if I'd never noticed it was glass
but all he did was glare at me
a Fury in a nightgown

then turn and step away
which is when I see myself
dropping cross-legged to the floor
rocking and weeping
when in fact I took the steps

two at a time and swerved
into the kids' room to stare
at their night-light
the little wooden house
that was mine as a child

a candy cottage edged by firs
and off to one side
the delicate cut-outs
of a boy and a girl drawn
by the windows' honeyed blaze

14 • *February Morning*

February Morning

I was standing in the bedroom
looking out at our neighborhood
winter sky striped pink and blue
the lawn the street the houses
just beginning to glow

an ordinary morning
like ten thousand other mornings
I'd viewed from this window
still its beauty startled me
and I felt sad to think

how little beauty matters
when suffering is commonplace
and vanishing unstoppable
it was as if I could see our life
from far above

or maybe from the future
the hour already gone
the day gone the room gone
and the scene itself a bright scrap
flaring in your hand

15 • *Threshold*

Threshold

When the house was first ours
before it smelled of paint and wax
before we'd laid down rugs
or cooked a single meal
in its small outmoded kitchen

it had the stony scent
of shade under a garden shed
the damp unsettled smell
of quiet and disuse
though it hadn't stood empty

we'd open the back door
and there it was
intractable as loneliness
or the memory of loneliness
as if someone else's loss

were lodged within our gain
and it seemed important
it seems important now
that before we moved in
the house smelled stony

and shadowed even in the light
of a mild November
as we crossed the threshold
ten twelve twenty times with tools
and tiles and cleaning supplies

each bright room blank
the walls and windows bare
steps uncarpeted floorboards scarred
but how sure I felt how safe
as if the history of this place

had always been leading
to the home we'd make
the home we were making
that weirdly balmy fall
when a life seemed long

16 • *Late at Night the Lightning*

Late at Night the Lightning

It must have been March
because the snow was surprising
though not as surprising
as the thunder and lightning
that woke us and woke our son

a three-year-old who asked
Is it moon lightning or star lightning
and we had no idea
none of it seemed real
even when we caught the scene

in shuddering flashes
wet snow bending boughs
and breaking great branches
which dropped to the street
and slid or shattered

why were we enchanted
instead of feeling threatened
did the beauty of the storm
conceal its danger
who knows how long it lasted

we didn't stay up to watch
and now the story seems embellished
the backlit cascading flakes
more wonder than weather
our son at the window an image

not a boy and the room
this very room where I sit
to remember where I sit to invent
not a place but a time
I've conjured and for what

17 • *Mockingbird*

Mockingbird

. . . singing uselessly, uselessly all the night.

—WALT WHITMAN

In place of the world
dark now and otherwise silent
this spiraling birdsong
chewks and down-slurred whistles
chirps and trills and whirrs

three rising notes three times
then three fluting warbles
not a chorus
but a single bird
showing off his range

how beautiful I thought at first
waking to the sound
and hours later it goes on
as if this mockingbird alone
would animate the empty night

in place of the world
nest and sky
and May leaves pivoting
a tranced-out parody
something like desire

18 • *A Marriage*

A Marriage

We were separate and inseparable
which doesn't mean we were together
all the time in fact for years
you were away ten days each month
but that never mattered

we'd say our house our kids our life
we were in all of it together
the holidays the drudgery we danced
and raked and planted we scoured
the tub folded the children's clothes

we sat beside our parents' sickbeds
and then beside each other's
walking hospital hallways side by side
after sleeping or not sleeping
after waking in the dark terrified

and weak though most of the time
we were at home where sometimes
we'd argue about small things
that we knew to be large things
the largest things our differences

distressing and exciting us
proud of one another with private joy
disappointed with private sorrow
what else could marriage be
though before we met I thought love

might be some form of recognition
a way of seeing through
the illusion of separateness
which was what he thought too
(you know who I mean)

when he said all those years ago
Just now when I kept my eyes closed
I was thinking of you without your body
I was thinking we've taken off each other's bodies
the way we've taken off each other's clothes

a wish or a lie but either way
it wasn't long before you and I
began a deeper story
strange to imagine now
how separate our lives once were

19 • *Echo*

Echo

All the years we spent
expecting years to come
no thought of last things
each spring another spring
new grass at our feet

it was April it was May
we sat out back at sunset
spread a map across our knees
to plot a summer route
but I was never good at that

I struggled to make sense
of distances and altitudes
the skewed concentric circles
where mountains must be
I had to squint to picture

the valleys and our figures
stepping stone by stone
across each ink-blue line
the map itself a paper world
complete with its own key

while the real world's mysteries
kept unfolding
how tender and deliberate
and hopeful we were then
how tireless and baffled

climbing months like switchbacks
you and I with the children
behind and then beside us
and now so far ahead
shouting at a rock face

to hear their ghosts shout back
the voices theirs
or almost theirs
and then unrecognizable
except as falling human sounds

20 • *The Near and Far*

The Near and Far

How it felt then to walk into the yard
before the children were awake the dark
starting to lift and the wet grass cold
under the soft leaves our sugar maple
dropped beside the bench where I sat

in my nightgown and my shabby robe
"surveying my kingdom" what a joke
our garden a patchy mess the bushes
and flowers we'd planted shaded out
by trees we planted later still I loved

to sit there on the first cold mornings
when the children were young and I
was almost never alone just to sit
and stare back at the yard the house
the early hour colorless a dreamscape

separate from the garish hoop of days
weeks months careening past us
a blur of playing fields and schoolyards
office market library the holidays
the injuries those years when we were

lucky and unlucky happy and overbooked
waking eating rushing off to what came
next it was a long list and sometimes
I couldn't keep up but what I think of now
sitting on our bench the children grown

the garden neat the morning unscripted
what I think of now isn't home but away
our yellow tent in scrublands and forests
on bluffs above the ocean all the summers
we backpacked as a family but mostly

of the time we crossed a valley floor littered
with obsidian the sunlight glinting off
the glassy chips beneath our boots
you and I and our boy and our girl
that August in the wilderness in Oregon

where the next day or the next we reached
a snowfield at dusk the one we had to cross
to find our campsite by a lake but it was crazy
to take a chance the snow icing up
what if the children slipped and tumbled

down that slope it was so steep so far
but you weren't afraid you broke trail
kicked your heels through the scaly snow
made tracks for us to follow the sky
above the mountains swanking orange

then pink then purple as each of us placed
one boot after another into the steps
you'd fashioned and it didn't take forever
it was only a few minutes until the ice
gave way to slush the grass reappeared

and there we were at twilight giddy
with relief dropping our heavy packs
whooping in triumph though my legs
were shaking when you passed the flask
and the first sip of brandy blazed

on my tongue I don't know why
that evening keeps coming back
maybe because I was terrified crossing
what must have been a glacier
however small however thin

it was blue at the edges wasn't it blue
our common tracks blue and yet we made it
we made it we were safe we pitched our tent
we built a fire pine logs snapping
camp-stove humming in that circle of sight

beyond which the children flickered
far and farther off shouting or singing
headlong through the dark
in their long johns their jackets
their bright winter hats

Jody Bolz received her undergraduate and graduate degrees from Cornell University, where she studied with A.R. Ammons. Her poems have appeared widely in such literary magazines as *The American Scholar, North American Review, Ploughshares, Poetry East, Prairie Schooner,* and *The Women's Review of Books*—and in a number of anthologies, including *Her Face in the Mirror: Jewish Women on Mothers and Daughters* (Beacon Press), *Don't Leave Hungry: Fifty Years of Southern Poetry Review* (University of Arkansas Press), and *Ghost Fishing: An Eco-Justice Poetry Anthology* (University of Georgia Press). Bolz worked as a writer and editor for both The Wilderness Society and The Nature Conservancy, taught creative writing for more than twenty years at George Washington University, and served as executive editor of *Poet Lore,* America's oldest poetry journal, from 2002 to 2019. Her most recent book of poetry is the novella-in-verse *Shadow Play* (Turning Point, 2013).

PRAISE FOR *SHADOW PLAY*

"An extraordinary act of literary ventriloquism.... The poem, in all its formal inventiveness and variety, is an incarnation of the ineluctable passage of time itself." —VIKRAM CHANDRA

"Bolz's book is more than a page-turner.... In quiet, affirming moments, she gives us a fresh appreciation of love's fragility and the enduring strength of desire." —FRANK BECK

"*Shadow Play* explores a failed early marriage in an altogether original way, combining the momentum of memoir with the music of poetry.... *What sense will you make of the heart's slow progress?*, Bolz asks, even as she shows us the answer." —LINDA PASTAN

"There is a hard-won stillness at the center of this book, the kind of stillness a reader finds when a fine poet has figured things out and hasn't been crushed by the discovery." —CORNELIUS EADY

"Part-travelogue, part-memoir, part-theatre, but fiction by definition, *Shadow Play* is a spellbinding read...pure poetry, trope-filled with beautifully crafted lines of readable free verse that tell a compelling story." —ANNE HARDING WOODWORTH

"Bolz handles the short lines with brio, wringing from them narration brimming with energy and speed, lyric moments of limpid melancholy, and dialogues that span sarcasm and incredulity, complicity and hurt. The formal pressure of these poems is extraordinary." —LEE ROSSI

"Moving from present to past, from recollected conversations to invented ones that take place in the present, Bolz manages a multi-layered discourse, combining gorgeous lyric poems with colloquial, floating dialogues." —ROBIN BECKER

“Which of us hasn't been tormented with thoughts of someone we loved long ago? ‘I shall tell you of the first root of our love,’ says Francesca to Dante in Canto v of his ‘Inferno.’ *Shadow Play* explores such longing between a sensible married woman and a ghost from when she was young, backpacking through Asia.” —JOHN BALABAN

“Meditative and passionate, *Shadow Play* works its way toward an approximate answer to the question it opens with, a quotation from Roland Barthes: ‘How does a love end? Then it does end?’” —JASON DEYOUNG

“[Bolz's] clean, clear lyrics attempt the move through desperation to understanding. What poetic policies are involved? Certainly redemption, for what else could the past possibly be for?” —GRACE CAVALIERI